Joyous Grace:
My Soul's Journey Started Here

Shernise Alexa Allen

Order this book online at www.trafford.com
or email orders@trafford.com

Most Trafford titles are also available at major online book retailers.

Printed in the United States of America.

ISBN: 978-1-4907-4501-5 (sc)
ISBN: 978-1-4907-4502-2 (hc)
ISBN: 978-1-4907-4500-8 (e)

Library of Congress Control Number: 2014915063

Trafford rev. 07/02/2014

 www.trafford.com

North America & international
toll-free: 1 888 232 4444 (USA & Canada)
fax: 812 355 4082

Contents

SADNESS/DESPAIR

GRATITUDE

JOY

LOVE LOST / LOVE

GIVING

STRUGGLE / COURAGE

AND IN THE END...

Foreword

Putting these poems together to form this book has been a long journey in itself. Now, at last, I see the dream realized. It was hard not to edit some poems to reflect my current state of consciousness. As the book title states, these poems are from the first part of my journey in this lifetime.

Acknowledgements

As Soul, on the road to becoming a true co-worker with God, I believe I have lived many lifetimes in order to truly appreciate God's love for all life.

This has not been a solo journey. I want to thank my family and my close friends who are my family for loving me so unconditionally.

I promise to share more of my journey in future installments. I love poetry. It has been my saving grace to help me express sadness, sheer joy, and every emotion in between.

IN THE BEGINNING...

A poet

I was given the gift
of poetic verse
of rhyme, and line and meter
so that I could
express strong emotions
though I really am quite meager.

And they listen
to my pencil
which writes verse as a gift from God
'stead of singing
or dancing, or speaking
my poems do the job.

Yes it flows from me
like music
of nature's smallest singing birds
with my mouth
in utter silence
they can still listen to my words.

DREAMS

To Be (inspired by Thoreau)

There will be days
when everyone forms a straight line
only to find you making circles.

And you find yourself whistling
an aria on a crowded bus
where silent people's only concern
is getting home from work.

To be labeled
"strange" for wearing that layered look
that makes you look like a child
from Godspell on Broadway - or worse...

Or called a flower child
for loving to roll in the autumn leaves
and for picking a bouquet of dandelions
to give to little babies as they go by
in their strollers out for a Sunday walk.

So you walk up the hill backwards
so that people can see your face
when you talk to them.

Though your pace
may not befit others
continue to be...

To be warmed by visions
of the future and
don't be stifled
by the cold grip of reality.

Wondering to some far off land
of your dreams
that exists in peace and serenity.
Don't let your dreams be shattered
because someone steps on your toes.

Go forth! And
write songs that
no one else can sing
for you only
can hear the music
and know the words....

Never for too long

Meeting people's faces
always moving on
from one place to another
never for too long.

Glimpsing at the living,
silence for the dead
reverence in the churches
nothing need be said.

The memories I've made they go so fast.
Oh how this has changed me.
I must stop to rearrange me
before moving on ---
       never for too long.

Traveling thru the flatlands,
thru the rolling hills,
up and down high mountains
with sights to give you chills.

I know that I'll forget things
but I don't feel so sad.
The experience has changed me
and for that I am glad.

Missing home but loving this carefree life.
The culture fascinates me.
The train rides that sedate me,
'cause some are very long—
Always moving on.

Self-reflection Series: A wish fulfilled

With touch that heals
  and laughing eyes
    a kiss,
      a warm caress.

A long lost feeling
  fills my heart
    with love so sensuous.

My brooding sadness
  swept away
    replaced
      by joy and love.

His presence
  is a blessing —
    sent
      from up above.

GOD

Gifts

to an open mind
   God gives knowledge.

to a hungry mouth
   God provides food.

a wondering soul
   God guides with Truth.

on a sleepless night
   God shines a star.

to a lonely one
   God is a friend.

on a stormy day
   God sent a rainbow.

in the early morn
   God lets birds sing.

to cheer you up
   God made a smile.

for those who dream
   God created clouds.

an open heart
   God fills with Love.

Gracious Miracles

God works slow
    and gracious miracles.

Gently changing you
    to blend with time.

So with a subtle
    twitch of the eye

A better person
    you'll be come.

And though these changes
    may be slight

They sum to make
    a greater difference.

So if along this path
    of betterment

By chance you notice
    God's guiding hand.

Don't forget to give thanks
    for this help received along the way.

The Razor's Edge

I believe
in going beyond
what can be seen

To explore
with senses
long dormant

To reach out
and travel
beyond the mind

To experience
what words
cannot express...
your true self,
and still further...
Love
and thought Love...
God.

FRIENDSHIP

Self-reflection Series: Death of friendship

I thought that we were friends.
You said you'd always care,
and that no matter what,
you would still be there.

To celebrate the good times
to sooth me when I'm sad.
But it seems that something I have said
has made you very mad.

So now you do not speak to me
you seem not much to care.
Have I hurt your feelings oh so much
that you must pretend that I'm not there?

That I no longer exist to you
erased right from your mind
like chalk dust on a black board.
You used to be so kind.

What happen to that loving friend
that I had grown to know?
What have I done to cause you pain
enough to let me go?

A poem (for a friend)

A word
> to help console and mend broken hearts
>> left from shattered dreams.
> to give assurance
>> and lend courage.

A hand
> to hold trembling,
> to join us as one.
> to strengthen the bonds of friendship;
>> you are never alone in the world.

A face
> that smiles, laughs, sparkles, and glitters,
> yet at times is filled with tears and sorrow
> but ever showing true emotion.
>> for between the two of us there is nothing to hide.

A memory
> of togetherness,
> of what two can accomplish more than one alone.
> a living catalog of experiences in our minds
>> to cherish for years to come.

A poem
> for the many hours of friendship
> so that in some respects
> we will never part.

footprints in the sand

He was from a land far away,
  a mysterious but gentle face to fill my dreams.

A friend that came like the foaming tide
  that barely chanced to wash my shore,
     only to leave in the blink of an eye...
Never to be seen again?

So as my new friend drifts from shore,
  I tearfully stand and wave good-bye.

For he has left his footprints in the sand.
And though the next tide threatens
        to wash them away,
the impression he made
  will forever remain nestled
      in my mind.

LOSS

Rejoice in Life

Family,
The energy of unity
the faith that bind blood together.

With love
that underlies all
enduring all manner of war, argument, pain.

Death,
that breaks the circle
disrupts the unity
releasing energy into unclaimed space.

a breath,
       a pause,
              a tear,
                     a sigh,
                            a prayer – all is calm.

In silence,
that is filled with self-reflection
mourning the present,
       cherishing the past,
              hoping for the future.

Reunited in faith
the circle now rejoined ---
       closer, for the loss of one.

Untitled *

* in memory of Hattie Belle Woods Spearman

Momma,
I miss you.

I miss the good times we had.
I miss your ever constant
      Devotion to me.

I know you're happy where you are
getting that long deserved rest...
      the hard way.

I know I'll really have to
      grow up now.
No more gentle nudges,
No more shoulder to lean on.
I am on my own now ----
But I am a little scared
and my heart is lonely.

I guess I'll learn to live without you
but it won't be easy,
your departure has left a big void in my identity.
I'm still numb, momma.
When will I feel again?

There's no one whom I can feel as I
      felt with you.
That gentle balance of hate and love,
      respect and envy,
            a swaying pendulum ---
but you're leaving has left me no balance at all.

I've won the tug-of-war
The battle, our battle
but winning doesn't mean happiness.
I would have preferred victory thru understanding.

So many things I wanted to say but couldn't
yet I said, "I love you.", and
your reply, "I love you, too"
      has made everything alright between us.

Truce --- Peace at last.
So sleep in peace, momma.
Rest.
Let God take care of you ---
      no one else could.

"M"

Today I lost a friend
    who chose to leave this world, some say early.
But Soul knew
    the lessons of this life were done.
His life, this life
    was brief, but meaningful,
        short, but full of life's lessons,
            full of love.
For he cared about many,
    he cared for many,
 perhaps more than he cared for himself.
    For that, I am sad.
Yet now I'm sure
    he knows, as he's looking down upon us,
how much he was loved.

HOPE

With life, there is hope.

If every door is closed to me,
I must find an open window
     to crawl to my freedom
     or I'll rot inside myself.

For there is still hope to feed on
 It keeps me alive while I'm trapped
   in the dungeon of my own misdeeds.
With dreams to give me fresh air to breath
 when the stale air of this inner tomb
   has closed me to the rest of the world.

And it is faith that tells me
 there'll be a lighthouse on some distant shore
   to shine a light into the misty fog
   and guide me from my trouble waters
   so that I won't drown.

There's No Rain without a Rainbow

There are times
  when I am lonely
  when the hurt's
  within myself and
  I've tried and tried
  so many times
  to put it on the shelf.

I cry away my sorrows.
  I laugh away my tears.
  For if sadness rains upon my life
  a rainbow will appear.

Like after barren Winter
  comes fresh and flowery Spring
  I see my life as seasons
  and with each
  challenge brings.

I'm not a weeping willow
  nor am I a sturdy tree.
  I've learned that life
  is filled with strife
  and lessons to strengthen me.

I fly a kite of freedom.
  Sing praises to the air.
  For life it seems
  without a dream
  would be a solemn affair.

There's no rain without a rainbow.
  no Winter without Spring.
  Those simple thoughts
  stay with my heart
  giving strength to me again.

Seeds of Love

The Seed of Love
  is planted in each of us.

But like any other seed
  some sprout a little
    some bloom and then wither
      still others grow and blossom.

It is our responsibility
  to find the food, the nourishment ---
    the right mixture of life experiences
That make that seed of love
  bloom and grow within us.

For it is those well-nourished blossoms that will burst open
  scattering more seeds of love to the winds
Thus creating a meadow of love
  where once there was just one flower.

SADNESS/
DESPAIR

Image

Moonbeams
make the crystal pond
glitter
      and sparkle
there...
as a single tear
falls
shattering my moonlit image
making rings
in perfect symmetry ...
and slowly,
my broken visage
is pieced back together
by some invisible, patient
guiding hand
leaving me
to gaze
at my sad reflection
once
  again....

Oh What A Waste

my life isn't worth two cents.
just like scrap metal —
wasted.
broken glass that's jagged.
i've stabled those
i love most so many times
there's no more blood to bleed
red like an angry sunset or mysterious dawn.

what more can i do?
in my brief encounter with living
i've managed to destroy
everything i sought to build.
fallen bricks,
broken pillars,
there's nowhere left to stand.
look at those poor people
trapped
hurt and
permanently damaged
beneath my ruins:
junk,
   trash,
      filth,
my life —
oh what a waste.

Self-reflection Series: Living in Sadness

Living in sadness,
Living with fear,
Life without happiness
no laughter here.

Living through changes
life seems to deal
more sadness than happiness
for me to feel.

Trying to think positive
and eliminate doubt.
The struggle is endless;
there seems no way out.

Tired of living,
too scared to die.
Hopeless confusion —
What next do I try?

Somewhere inside me
there must be some good
that somehow or other
got misunderstood.

My wish for the future ---
just to survive,
so that tomorrow I'll wakeup
and know I'm alive.

Living in the Eye of the Storm

As life's turmoil
 swirls around you,
don't forget the
 "blessing of the eye of the storm".

For inside yourself,
 if you look,
you will find that
        calm, peaceful,
                neutral center: Soul –
        always there,
                always aligned with God.

Silent, Serene Eternity

One night
    we sat and talked to the stars
    so far away
    in the black velvet night -
    stars that shown like pen-lights flickering...

And we smiled back at the moon:
    a friend to us eternally,
    cousin to our mother Earth,
    so yellow-white and big and round...

And we thanked God for these moments,
    where with silence is eternity,
    with togetherness, friendship and love
    to add warmth to these memories
    we will cherish -
        forever....

New Freedom

You

      opened new horizons
      so I could expand;

      let loose the door
      so I could unfold;

      stepped aside
      so I could walk my path;

      and now that I know where it leads
      I walk straight and tall without a crutch.

All of this because of you.

JOY

Let Us Fly

Write a book.
Fly a plane.
Race cars.
Walk a lane.

I can do anything
        anytime
                anywhere.
Forget my troubles
Excuse your cares.
Come fly with me
To the soaring summits
        Of our imagination.
Let us enter a portal and
        Emerge in a world of violent passions
with wild beasts
        and savage kings,
                Koo-ca-tow birds
                        with peacock wings

Let us fly upward
and when we reach
what seems a peak.
Let us not be frightened, less we be weak,
But swoop upward
In leaps and bounds
Let us have courage
to achieve our wildest dreams
and after
Let us go still further
And pray we never, ever reach the top

Let us fly!

Winter Piece

Winter wind whistling thru myself
while the warm sun shines from far above
to melt the snow
so early crocus can bloom.

The footprinted snow that I must travel
spells destination bound with every step
no one wavers from the path.

Church bells fill the mountain wind;
sleigh bells sound from the valley below.
Whistling wind and noiseless silence
 complete the symphony of sound.
Music here and all around.

I see a snow angel,
   not my creation, but delicate none the less.
I can smell the burnt warmth of a fireplace nearby
as the snowy lace begins to fall again.

Joyeux

Le ciel est clair et perpetual
et moi, je suis un oiseau dans le ciel.
Ni vente, ni pluie quand je voie.
Je puis aller pour jamais.

English Translation:

Joyous

The sky is clear and endless
And I, I am a bird in the sky.
No wind, no rain as I fly.
I could go on forever.

LOVE LOST /
LOVE

He loves me not

I used to think my life was a rose,
red with long stem symbolizing beauty,
                honestly,
                      elegance –
                            a thing of nature.

Then I fell in love
  and put all my trust in my rose to tell me
If he loved me –
  Only to find
        he loved me not.
Now I have no love,
  and my life,
            my pretty red rose
                has become tiny, wilted petals
                        in my hand.

They feel so moist and cool,
  while their scent brings back fond memories….

I pondered long their destiny
  and after thought
I carefully
  threw the petals away
                    one
                          by
                      one.

It's My Loss

We started with a bang —
but I guess it was just the sound of our balloon bursting,
and with it any hopes of friendship.

I feel so helpless -
Like a child after knocking over Mommy's precious china vase.
It has splintered into a million pieces,
and I am unable
   even to sweep up the smallest part.
   (for fear I might cut myself and bleed to death).

How could I let something as precious as you
slip thru my hands
to break on the hard cement into so many pieces?
My heart has broken too.

For my brief experience of you
   was like champagne.
You went to my head;
 You made my eyes sparkle;
   You made me laugh and see a deeper self;
    You gave me profound new courage, and in the end
I reached for you - only
   because of my drunken stupor
I missed,
   knocking you off that pedestal
                        to fall and break....

So here I am,
  cursing my clumsiness,
         dreading tomorrow's hangover,
                        and weeping...
      over the loss of you.

Possibly in another world

If things were slightly different
He could love me.
He would take my hand
and we could run along a sandy beach.
We could laugh together
and share our secrets that seem so dear.
We could sing a song of silent notes
as we snuggle close near a burning fire.
And if things were slightly different,
he could caress me openly.
He could speak what I know are his silent thoughts
and no one would call him a fool for loving me.
I could look into his gentle eyes
And see his new found treasure - me.
But here is now.
And when I look at him,
he dares not even smile.

A moment's time

He was a familiar stranger.
Yet he held me close and tight that night.
I felt so wanted in his arms
  that stoked my shoulders, back and neck.
So gentle was his sweet caress
no words were needed, none were spoken
  for ours was the language of touch;
a silent but intimate way to say, "I care for you."
And when he stopped I kissed his lips and
  took his large warm hands in mine
    to kiss each finger one by one in silence.
And in return he kissed my mouth long and full
until we blended into one....
After as we sat intertwined
I could feel the gentle rhythm of his breathing
  and his heartbeat slow and steady.
With the warmth of his body, he encircled me.
  such was my contentment ----
Then it came time to say farewell.
With tight embrace we said goodbye.
Knowing we'd never meet again;
  but realizing that
This was our one moment in time;
To share what never before had been,
To remember what never again could be.

Forever & Always, with love

Our love for each other had spanned many years;
  together we both have grown.
We know each other like two best friends
  for together we're never alone.

Though it hasn't been all happiness,
  rarely a word of complaint will you hear.
For we both know what we have is special
  to have lasted for so many years.

So in the spirit of love and friendship,
  let us celebrate in a special way.
Happy Anniversary! My love, my partner,
  may our hearts join as one again today.

Untitled

My kind and gentle teddy bear
　You make me feel so secure, so happy;
　You listen to me laugh and cry;
　You feel my every mood and understand.

I'm a child again with you.
　A child in that I trust you completely
　I stand wide-eyed with wonder
　　at your every move;
　You're just too perfect to be true.

But there you are ---
　In my mind and in my soul.
　Apart from me but part of me.
　Hugging you just makes me feel stronger.

Can you feel my love?
　Of course you can, but even still.
　I love you so much it scares me.
　For you have stepped from my dreams into reality.

I no longer have to say, "I wish..."
　Because you are here --- now,
　And you have fulfilled so many of my wishes,
　That I know dreams really can come true.

GIVING

Given from the Heart

The Heart of God
  right at the core
that has always existed
that will endure
that spark inside each and
        every Soul is Love.

But Soul must learn to share the Love
  for it must be detached,
            yet radiant
        like the warming sun.
It must be given to
        everything and to everyone.

Just one act of love

It takes just one
      act of love
   to turn a life around
Unfolding situations, one by one
     until the heart is radiant
        with love's golden glow.
And life's melancholy melodies
     modulate in each refrain
        with notes charged with vibrant resonance
  launching echo
     after echo of Love in waves.

Heaven in Your Heart

There must be Heaven in your heart
   for that is where God's music starts
Sung with the breath of Love,
   from Soul, let lyrics flow.

Through simple acts of philanthropy
   one by one given without thought....
That is the only way to God —
   Give from the heart.

Thinking of Self will not do.
   There're too many tough times to go through.
All life is cause and effects
   with debts we must pay.

Now more than ever we must share
   Love without question or pause.
It's not too late, for humanity's sake —
   Give from the heart!

STRUGGLE /
COURAGE

Waterfall

Waterfall
I'm falling or is it that I fly
Trust
If I could only trust
Fear be gone
I must move on
Go with the flow
Waterfall
Am I here in the now?
What's the next step?
Why must I think?
Trust
If I could only trust
I must move on
Go with the flow
Waterfall

Once Upon a Time Gone Dim

There was a time
when I would have conquered the world
Poverty, politicians, disease, hate, prejudice
  Gloom, misery, agony, despair...
All tidily wrapped in one neat bundle
tied with string and buried so deep within the ground
that pressure and heat
would consume them in flame....
But now
my conquering instincts
have become numb.
I'd rather nestle in sweet conformity
safe from the anxiety
  of a conqueror's dream
  with the fear or nightmare of defeat.
Yes, I'd rather
roll out of bed to face another day –
same as the last, same as the next,
then bolt upright in the middle of the night
with eyes staring into the cold chilling blackness
awaiting the promised attach
of the silent, but ever-present enemy...
I've put away my youthful dream
of conquering the world.
I accept it as it is;
  it could be better, yes, but then again –
  it could easily be much, much worse.

All I Ask

When I look at you, my friend
I do not look for color,
  I look for personality —
   a mouth that smiles or frowns,
   eyes that sparkle or cry, a turned up nose
   or wrinkled brow.
I look for the emotional expression and
  hands that move with every gesture.
Creativeness is what I enjoy about you,
  your unique way of saying, "I'm me!".
I listen to your joyful dreams
  and learn from your experiences.
Together we can share
  so much and form a bond with will remain.
Even if we both have
  secrets that we don't confide
I'll never ask for anything
  more from you
than I would ask of myself -
  no one is perfect.
Just don't pull me down, my friend,
  by one seeing just my color.
I am not to be branded like some cow.
I am one of God's unique creations: Soul.
And though I don't expect you to understand
I merely ask you to respect me
  as a fellow Soul.
For if you do that,
  I can truly consider you to be my friend
And from that moment on
  we both will grow.

AND IN THE END...

The Way is Love

There is no other way but love
   God's love
      the kind that burns deep
         beyond the heart to the core, to Soul.

Love that stirs within us
   a longing,
      a hunger,
         a need for Home.

For it is Divine Love that sustains us
   without IT
      we and everything else in the universes
      would cease to exist.

Love that touches that
   spark of God in each of us
that spark which is kindled
   by the breath of the Holy Word
      until it burns like Holy Fire
      consuming us in IT:
Nothing can stop the way of Love.